STAY FOR THE CUP OF COFFEE

How to Support Others in Grief

ALAN D. WOLFELT, PH.D.

Companion
PRESS

© 2024 by Alan D. Wolfelt, Ph.D.

Companion Press is an imprint of the Center for Loss and Life Transition, 3735 Broken Bow Road, Fort Collins, Colorado 80526.

29   28   27   26   25   24   6 5 4 3 2 1

ISBN: 978-1-61722-333-4

WELCOME

When I was growing up, my family
attended a Methodist church.

After the Sunday service, we'd join the rest of the
parishioners for social hour. We gathered in a large,
open room filled with tables and folding chairs.
While the kids ran around and played, the
grown-ups chatted and sipped coffee from
Styrofoam cups. Besides coffee, there were
other refreshments, like lemonade or Kool-Aid,
cookies, and, often, doughnuts.

This was staying for the cup of coffee.

During that era, many other community events also included staying for the cup of coffee. At the close of baseball games and other sporting events, we could count on treats and beverages. After holiday dinners, family and friends shared dessert and coffee. When the last notes of the school concert faded to applause, you guessed it—coffee and cookies. And after a funeral, there was always, always a luncheon (think ham sandwiches and tuna casseroles), dessert, and coffee.

It was only as I got older that I really learned to appreciate staying for the cup of coffee. It's such a simple but meaningful ritual. It's an informal time of community and conversation. It's no-pressure face time. It's really just being together without distractions. The formal events (church service, meeting, dinner, concert, funeral) have finished, and the coffee hour, as it is often called, ushers in a sigh of relaxation and a few minutes of unstructured but intimate camaraderie.

This is the spirit of staying for the cup of coffee with the grieving people in your life. Coffee isn't a requirement, but relaxed presence is.

You are simply there with the grieving person to listen as they talk about whatever they want to talk about and to hold space for whatever thoughts and feelings they may experience and express.

I've been a grief counselor and educator for 40 years now. In today's busy and technology-driven world, staying for the cup of coffee is much less common. Yet it's still just as—if not more, given its rarity—meaningful. That's why I wrote this book—to help us all remember how to be there for people who are suffering after a loss. In fact, my grief counseling model, which I call companioning, is based not on "treating" grief but on the art of being compassionately present to mourners.

When you're wondering how to support someone who's grieving, I hope you'll pick up this book for reminders and inspiration. Flip to any page, allow the content to guide you into a staying-for-the-cup-of-coffee mindset, then reach out to the grieving person.

Your presence and listening ears are so needed. Bring coffee and doughnuts.

Being a good friend in grief is about
staying for the cup of coffee.

But what does that mean?
It's quite simple, really.

Staying for the cup of coffee
means spending some

EXTRA QUALITY TIME

with the grieving person.

Companionship and conversation
will flow, though they may or may
not be centered on the loss.

In Sweden, people routinely drop whatever they are doing—often in the middle of the afternoon—and gather with friends or family for coffee and a snack.

This ritual is called fika—

pronounced FEE-kuh.

Fika is a social activity. It provides a simply structured routine for people to get together, relax, and catch up with each other. It fosters communication and bonding as well as individual mental health.

The art of fika is a nice model for supporting someone in grief: meeting up often and informally, even if just for a few minutes, to be present to one another and to normalize talking about whatever needs to be talked about.

"Too often we underestimate
the power of a touch, a
s_mi_le,
a kind word, a listening
e
a
r,
an honest compliment, or the
⟩ smallest ⟨
act of caring,
all of which have the potential
to turn a life around."

— Leo Buscaglia

Humans are social creatures. We need each other. In fact, it's our relationships with one another that give our lives the most meaning and joy.

But with the rise of digital technology, we're more separated from one another than ever before. We can be in the same room with others yet rarely speak to them.

GRIEF SUPPORT REQUIRES PRESENCE.

Texts, emails, and phone calls are often good additions to the mix, but it's impossible to replace face-to-face time.

As much as you can, be present to the grieving person.

A COUPLE OF DEFINITIONS

**GRIEF is everything we think and feel
inside of ourselves after a loss.**
Living with deep grief is painful,
but it is way more painful when we
don't have outlets for our grief.

**Sharing our grief outside of ourselves
is called MOURNING.**
Mourning is what gives our grief movement and
helps us integrate the loss over time.

When you sit and listen to someone who is
grieving, you're helping them mourn.

Bit by bit, day by day,
you're helping them heal.

WAYS TO SPEND AN HOUR

Watch a TV show

Do laundry

Scroll on your phone

Mow your lawn

Exercise

Pay bills

Keep working

Clean out your refrigerator

Get your tires rotated

Stop in to visit a grieving
friend or loved one

"Do what you can to show you care about other people, and you will make the world a better place."

— Rosalynn Carter

HOSPITALITY

is a big part of staying for the cup of coffee.

It's the friendly, generous welcoming
of friends and neighbors.

Hospitality focuses on the needs of others.
It ensures they feel welcome, special,
comfortable, and well cared for.

How can you create moments of hospitality
for the person who is grieving?

With:

PRESENCE   GENEROSITY
ATTITUDE   COMFORT
FOCUS   CAREGIVING

Food and drink are optional, but they're
almost always an appreciated touch.

Grieving people often feel like they're **going crazy** or that their grief is somehow abnormal.

You CAN AFFIRM THAT THEIR THOUGHTS AND FEELINGS ARE UNDERSTANDABLE AND NORMAL.

Yes, grief is a disruptive, challenging experience, and the thoughts and feelings it can create are also disruptive and challenging. But all those thoughts and feelings are also normal.

You might say something like:

"How natural for you to feel this way."

"You're not going crazy. You're grieving."

"There's nothing wrong with you. You're doing your best in a difficult situation."

"Nothing is more important than empathy for another human being's suffering. Nothing. Not career, not wealth, not intelligence, certainly not status. We have to feel for one another if we're going to survive with dignity."

— Audrey Hepburn

Staying for the cup of coffee is
slooooowww.

It takes time.

It's not rushed or task-oriented.

Grief itself is slow. Grief demands convalescence.

When possible, try not to feel pushed for time with the person who is grieving. Allow the encounter to unfold at their pace.

In between longer visits, it's good to stop by for quick check-ins. But try to find time for those unhurried sessions as well. They're an oasis in a stormy sea.

The art of presence is rare.
And it's getting rarer by the day.

Try to be there in person for your
friend who is grieving.

SHOW UP.

STEP UP.

DROP BY.

There doesn't need to be
an agenda. You don't need a
specific reason. Just...

BE THERE.

Whenever you're reaching out to or, especially, spending time with someone who's grieving, you're letting them know

a) you care
and
b) you're available to them.

As long as you communicate your openness to being compassionately present to anything they may want to express, you're doing your part. Even if they don't bring up or want to focus on the loss, you're still being a good friend in grief.

You don't always have to talk about the loss.

ANOTHER DEFINITION

DEEP LISTENING, also called active listening, means being fully present to the grieving person. It means listening with the intent not only to cognitively understand everything that is being said, but to *feel* what is being said.

It also means communicating your high degree of attention and focus back to the other person.

YOU PAY ATTENTION.

YOU LISTEN.

YOU AFFIRM WHAT YOU'VE HEARD.

YOU CONVEY YOUR COMPASSIONATE UNDERSTANDING.

Foundationally, relationships are built on trust.

The more available and steadfast you are in staying for the cup of coffee over time, the more the grieving person will trust that you care and are a reliable supporter.

You can be counted on.

Some people are open with
their feelings, while others are not.

If the grieving person you're reaching
out to support is an introvert or highly private,
they may be slow to open up to you.
They may also prefer that anything they tell
you be kept confidential.

Respect privacy.

LiSTEN = SiLENT

If you rearrange the letters in the word
"listen," you get "silent."

I hope you'll keep this serendipitous anagram in mind
whenever you stay for the cup of coffee.

Talk less, listen more. In fact, talk a lot less.
Don't feel compelled to fill gaps in the conversation with
chatter. Give the grieving person ample time and space
to express whatever is on their heart.

The more you make it clear that you are there to receive,
the more the griever will understand that they can open
up and fill the silence you've created for them.

I always try to remember:
Mouth closed. Ears open. Presence available.

"Listening is such a simple act. It requires us to be present, and that takes practice, but we don't have to do anything else. We don't have to advise, or coach, or sound wise. We just have to be willing to sit there and listen."

— Margaret J. Wheatley

ONE MORE DEFINITION!

The concept of "HOLDING SPACE" has become commonplace among counselors and other caregivers. Have you heard of it?

Holding space means to not only be present to someone who is struggling with a difficult life circumstance, but also to help make them feel safe and less alone as they learn to acknowledge their new reality and undergo their necessary transformation.

The grieving person is the driver, and we as supporters holding space for them are the passengers.

We accompany them sometimes. We let them choose where to go, how to go, and how quickly to go. We allow them to get lost. We bear witness without judgment to all of their thoughts and feelings, even really difficult ones. We help them trust in their own wisdom, pacing, and path.

"What does it mean to hold space for someone else? It means that we are willing to walk alongside another person in whatever journey they're on without judging them, making them feel inadequate, trying to fix them, or trying to impact the outcome. When we hold space for other people, we open our hearts, offer unconditional support, and let go of judgment and control."

— Heather Plett

Of course, staying for the cup of coffee isn't really about the coffee. It's about presence and empathy and hospitality.

Tea, soft drinks, water—they all work, too. Snacks or a simple meal are good.

No refreshments at all? That's fine, but do try to ensure that the grieving person is comfortable and feels well cared for.

THINGS TO SAY

"I'm sorry."

"I care about you."

"I wish you weren't having to
go through this."

"I'm good at _____
(listening, running errands, helping with
paperwork, hanging out, being a travel
companion, etc.). Please let me help."

"I've been thinking about you, and I want
to know how you're really doing."

"I want to be here for you."

Maya Angelou famously wrote, "People will forget
what you said, people will forget what you did, but
people will never forget how you made them feel."

THE NAME OF THE PERSON WHO DIED,
and the person they were, deserve a starring role in
your conversations with your grieving friend.

Don't be afraid to mention the person
who died. Loss and grief should never
be the elephant in the room.

Use the name of the person who died.
Grieving people often notice that others
avoid saying the name out of fear of
hurting them. But what's true more
often is that grieving people are hurt
that others pretend the death
didn't happen or don't bring
up the person who died.

Say the name.

Join the grieving person in remembering and
honoring the life.

STEPPING STONES

Show up

Be kind

Listen

Then

Over time

Marvel

As the path

Forward

Emerges

"So when you are listening to somebody, completely, attentively, then you are listening not only to the words, but also to the feeling of what is being conveyed, to the whole of it, not part of it."

— Jiddu Krishnamurti

GENEROSITY IS A BIG PART OF STAYING FOR THE CUP OF COFFEE.

After all, you're devoting your time and your attention. You're expending effort to create hospitality.

Ask yourself:

What is the most generous way in which I could help the grieving person right now?

Usually a grand gesture isn't what is needed. It's generally not the right moment to whisk the person away on an expensive trip, bring a lavish gift, or book reservations at a fancy restaurant.

Instead, think about giving generously of your presence, time, and empathy. Besides, those are always the greatest gifts of all.

Grieving people need safe spaces
in which they can be themselves.

It's often hard to mourn and live at the same time.

When you stay for the cup of coffee, you're fending
off the outside world for a short period of time.

YOU'RE CREATING A SHELTERED TIME AND SPACE IN WHICH THEY CAN FEEL SAFE AND UNDERSTOOD.

Since our culture isn't very good at
acknowledging and supporting grief,
many of us have never learned

how to talk to a grieving person.

But the truth is, it's easy. Starting a conversation
can be as simple as saying:

"I've been thinking about you."

Or:

"You've been on my mind and heart.
Let's get together for a cup of coffee."

Over coffee, conversation will flow naturally.

"Grief isn't an immediate problem
to solve but rather an unexplainable aspect
that stays in motion within a person.
When it strikes, it asks to be heard, felt,
but not necessarily understood.
It stands between light and shadow,
and in this in-between, we learn to live."

— J. Mike Fields

WHAT NOT TO SAY

"I know just how you feel."

"Other people have made it
through the same thing."

"You're strong. You'll be OK."

"I thought you'd be getting
over it by now."

"Life is hard."

"He wouldn't want you to be sad."

"You're lucky. Someone else I know..."

GRiEViNG PEOPLE
OFTEN FEEL HOPELESS.

Especially in the early months of their grief,
they may not be able to imagine a time that
they will ever feel better.

**But *you* have hope. You can
lend them some of yours.**

Be careful not to dismiss the necessity
of the pain of their loss. But when the
timing is right, you can also sprinkle some
hope. Hope is an expectation of a
good that is yet to come.

"I'm always going to be here for you."

"You have so many people who love and
want to care for you."

You are not responsible *for* others, but you are responsible *to* others.

Staying for the cup of coffee is one
of your responsibilities as a
friend and grief companion.

However, you are not responsible for
grieving people. They are ultimately
responsible for themselves.

Still, your regular, steady presence can be
among the essential stepping stones your
grieving friends need to get from
here to there.

"The human soul doesn't want to be advised or fixed or saved. It simply wants to be witnessed exactly as it is."

— Parker Palmer

WE'RE IN THIS
WORLD TOGETHER
FOR A REASON.

**TO LIFT EACH
OTHER UP.**

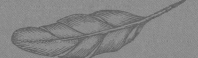

Every person you help

iS A PERSON WHOSE LiFE YOU'VE MADE BETTER.

66

Listening
is a positive act:
you have to put
yourself
out to do it.

99

— David Hockney

ABOVE AND BEYOND

The phrase "staying for the cup of coffee"
implies a little extra time and effort.

Let's say you drop off a meal for a grieving person.
That's a wonderful gift and show of support.
But if in addition to that you stay for the cup of coffee, that
means you carve out a few more minutes to be present to the
grieving person for an unhurried visit.

Likewise, if you see a grieving neighbor on the sidewalk or
run into a grieving colleague at the grocery store, the staying-
for-the-cup-of-coffee mindset encourages you not only to say
hello but also to stop and speak with them for a few minutes.
During your visit, you might also suggest getting together
another time for lunch or an actual cup of coffee. This
action will let them know you genuinely care.

**When you consider ways to "stay for the cup of coffee,"
one thing I hope you'll think about is the bonus time. You are
going above and beyond in some small way, giving a little
extra of your time and attention.**

HOW TO BE PRESENT TO SOMEONE YOU CARE ABOUT

Be there with them, in person if possible.

Set aside all distractions,
including your phone.

Be patient. Don't be in a hurry.

Use deep listening skills.

Perceive and attend to the
person's mood and needs.

Convey your empathy.

If you can't always be there in person

Maybe you want to support a grieving person who lives far away. Or maybe your life commitments prevent you from meeting in person often with the grieving person.

Video calls are the next best thing. After all, they still involve face-to-face time. Looking each other in the eye and being able to see body language go a long way toward conveying genuineness and empathy.

Voice calls are next on the list, followed by handwritten notes, texts, and emails. All methods of communication are appropriate and good, but when possible, face-to-face time is at the heart of supporting someone in grief.

"The friend who can be silent with us in a moment of despair or confusion, who can stay with us in an hour of grief, who can tolerate not knowing, not curing, not healing, and face with us the reality of our powerlessness, that is a friend who cares."

— Henri Nouwen

Being present to another's grief
might bring you to tears.

If so, go ahead and cry.

Don't be ashamed to cry. Crying is a natural way
of releasing stress chemicals in the body. Plus, tears
are a form of communication. They let others
know that we are feeling upset.

While you want to be careful not to overshadow the
griever's own grief—keeping the focus not on you but
on them—empathetic tears can also demonstrate
your deep listening and desire to help. You are with
the griever, even in the saddest moments.

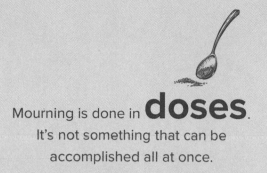

Mourning is done in **doses**.
It's not something that can be
accomplished all at once.

If you show up for your friend on a day
when they're not feeling like immersing themselves
in their grief, that's OK. It's their call what they
do or don't want to talk about.

Your friend may want to spend their time
with you taking a break from mourning.

When you next stay for the cup of coffee, however,
they might be ready for a dose of grief.

Your job is to be there no matter what happens.

As long as you can be counted on to be there for them,
your friend will come to trust that you can be turned
to in their next time of need.

People

Responding

Empathetically and

Showing up.

Everyone

Needs

Companionship and

Expression.

Spending time with someone who's grieving can be uncomfortable, especially if you're not a natural empath.

But the more you sit with discomfort, the more comfortable it becomes.

Challenging, big feelings are not only normal after a significant loss, they're necessary. They are central to what it means to be human. Staying for the cup of coffee is an important way to acknowledge this in your own life.

True life isn't virtual.

True life is real.

STAYING FOR THE CUP OF COFFEE IS DOING TRUE LIFE TOGETHER.

The art of presence isn't just about being physically there, in person.

It's also about accepting what happens in each moment and mindfully living in the now.

The Zen concept of **nonattachment to outcome** applies here. When we take meaningful action without worrying too much about the outcome of that action, we're doing what we can. Beyond that, we're surrendering the illusion of control.

As long as you stay for the cup of coffee, you don't have to stress about how your visits with the grieving person will go.

Be present, loving and listening. Then whatever happens, happens.

"Empathy is simply
listening, holding space,
withholding judgment,
emotionally connecting,
and communicating that
incredibly healing message
of 'you are not alone.'"

— Brené Brown

**It's actually not the
thought that counts.**

If you've been thinking about the
grieving person, that's good. That's a sign that
you're an empathetic human being.

But just thinking about (or praying for) the person
in grief isn't enough. Close the loop by letting them
know you're thinking about them.

Supporting someone who is grieving is a circle.
There needs to be ongoing two-way
communication and, ideally,
in-person interaction.

Relationships are built on three pillars

1.
PROXIMITY

Proximity means being there in person.

2.
FREQUENCY

Frequency means being in contact often.

3.
QUALITY TIME

Quality time means sharing activities that feel meaningful to both of you.

When you build up the three pillars with someone who is grieving, you are helping build a foundation of hope and healing.

WHAT NOT TO SAY

RELIGIOUS CONCEPTS

"God wouldn't give you any more than you can handle."

"They're in a better place."

"Now you have an angel in heaven."

"There's a reason for everything."

"It's God's will."

Sometimes grieving people look "fine." They may be going about their daily lives as usual. They may seem more or less the same when you run into them at the grocery store or see them at an event.

REMEMBER THAT APPEARANCES CAN BE DECEIVING.

Grief is invisible. The thoughts and feelings about the loss live deep inside the grieving person.

Lots of grieving people put on a mask when they're in public, especially after some time has passed. They can look normal on the outside but may still be devastated by grief on the inside.

Don't assume that the grieving person is "fine."
If a significant loss has torn them apart in the last few years, they're probably not "fine." They may have learned to compartmentalize when they need to, but they're still grieving, and they still need to express their grief.

> **"**
> Learning is a result
> of listening, which in
> turn leads to even
> better listening and
> attentiveness to the other
> person. In other words...
> we must have empathy,
> and empathy grows as
> we learn.
> **"**

— Alice Miller

ACTiVE LiSTENiNG SKiLLS

Active listening is a skill. You can learn it.
You can practice it. You can get better
and better at it.

**Using open body language—
eye contact, tone of voice, posture**

**Paraphrasing—repeating back what
you've heard but in your own words**

**Clarifying—asking questions to ensure
you understood what was said**

**Questioning—opening up new areas
of discussion with open-ended questions**

**Affirming—making it clear that the
person in grief is normal and loved**

"Most people do not listen with the intent to understand. They listen with the intent to reply."

— Stephen Covey

The famous anthropologist Margaret Mead was once asked what was the first sign of civilization in an early human culture.

She said it was a thigh bone that had been broken then healed.

The mended femur was a sign that the injured person had been tended to by others. This would have required feeding, sheltering, and protecting the injured person from danger for a period of weeks or months. Without this care, they would have died.

Staying for the cup of coffee is likewise civilized. Tend to your grieving friend over the coming months. Help them heal.

Have you ever noticed how our darker feelings have a bad reputation?

Sadness isn't pleasant, but in hard times, it's genuine. It's how life can be.

SAD iSN'T BAD.

Staying for the cup of coffee acknowledges that shock, numbness, fear, sadness, anger, and other challenging feelings are normal.

Love and friendship see us through both the hard times and the best times.

SHOWING UP

I'm not just thinking about you, I'm here.

FACE TO FACE

In the flesh.

MANO A MANO

How are you surviving?

Staying for the cup of coffee creates a pause in time.

It's a few unhurried minutes or hours with no pressure to say or do or accomplish anything.

The rest of the world keeps on keeping on, but the two of you are simply present to one another without concern for anything else.

Griefbursts

are sudden, intense expressions of emotion.
They can be difficult both for the grieving
person and for the observer.

Just remember that grief is often intense,
so it makes sense that the expressions of the grief
can also be intense. Sobbing, wailing,
and screaming are all normal.

If your friend has a griefburst in your
presence, that's OK.

You don't need to "do" anything.
Remain empathetic and calm.

Don't try to stop them
(unless they're hurting themselves or
others, or destroying property).

Let them know that it's safe for them to
express anything they need to.

"Crying does not indicate that you are weak. Since birth, it has always been a sign that you are alive."

— Charlotte Brontë

NO FIXING REQUIRED

Staying for the cup of coffee isn't about fixing someone else.

It's about being there and intently listening while they express anything they'd like to express.

If you have an impulse to offer advice or try to fix things, resist it. Just be there and offer your presence and empathy.

Grief is slow and recursive.

It demands convalesce.

There are no rewards for speed.

ONE SMALL ACT OF

KINDNESS

GOES A LONG WAY.

OFFER SINCERE PRAISE

"The funeral was really nice/meaningful."

"They were so lucky to have you in their life."

"You really loved her. I can tell you
still do and always will."

"You're being so open and honest
with your grief."

"Your friendship has been so
important to me."

"In allowing yourself to mourn,
I notice you are experiencing some
softening of your heart."

To accept and care for someone unconditionally means embracing them as they are.

In grief, people often think and act much differently than they normally would.

Of course they do! Grief is a shattering of a meaningful reality. There is debris everywhere. All change starts with chaos

When you stay for the cup of coffee and deeply listen and observe, you're signaling that you **ACCEPT** the grieving person's attitude, grooming, living conditions, struggles, and whatever they might say or do.

"A kind gesture
can reach a
wound that only
compassion
can heal."

— Steve Maraboli

THINGS NOT TO DO

DON'T give advice unless it's asked for.

DON'T visit once or twice then go away.

DON'T tell the other person that they
shouldn't feel what they feel.

DON'T try to calm or stifle the expression
of emotions. If someone in grief cries,
wails, or gets upset, it means they need
to cry, wail, or get upset.

DON'T offer your own stories of loss
(or those of others) unless they're asked for.

DON'T think you need to supply
answers or solutions.

You don't have to fill every
gap in the conversation.

In fact, moments of silence are healthy.

Sometimes people in grief need a moment to
collect their thoughts or reflect on a new insight.

Sometimes they just need time to cry or
even to sit with their feelings.

Sometimes they don't know what to say, and if you rush
in too soon with leading questions or comments, you
will end up directing their grief.

Yes, it can be uncomfortable to just be in silence.
But learning how to do it will
make you a better friend in grief.

OUTINGS MAY OCCUR

Sometimes staying for the cup of coffee might mean heading out somewhere together.

If the grieving person expresses that they could use some cheering up or fresh air, take them to do something they might enjoy. Examples include getting a pedicure together, visiting a museum, going fishing, walking through a natural area, or grabbing lunch at a favorite restaurant.

"Staying" doesn't have to mean staying home.

SiLENCE CAN BE SACRED.

When you remain quiet in the presence of
someone who is grieving, you are sustaining
an open heart and gentle spirit.

Consciously hush yourself and place trust
in the peace you help initiate.

Allow intentional silence to elevate the encounter
from the everyday to the spiritual.

As Henry David Thoreau said, "The tragedy begins
not when there is misunderstanding about words
but when silence is not understood."

Holding space for someone who is grieving means creating little bubbles in time and space for them to share anything they'd like to share.

When you create a bubble, the two of you are in it together. The demands of daily life are outside the bubble. Inside the bubble, there is nothing but time and freedom to feel and explore.

Your role is to make and safeguard the bubble, at least for a few minutes or an hour or two.

The role of the grieving person is to experience the safety and compassion inside the bubble, and to do and say whatever they want to during that time.

The word commiseration means
"to lament with."

When you stay for the cup of coffee,
you are signaling your willingness to
commiserate with the grieving person.

You're not there to pretend that everything's
fine or to model toxic positivity.

If the grieving person is feeling sad or angry or
upset or guilty, that's their reality. You're there
to commiserate, and in your commiseration,
to help them feel seen and affirmed.

Toxic positivity is an all-too-common attempt to gloss over difficult life circumstances.

"He wouldn't want you to cry."

"Other people have it worse."

"This too shall pass."

"Let's focus on the happy stuff."

Here are the corresponding truths:
Crying is helpful. Loss is not a competition.
Grief is hard and takes a really long time.
The sad stuff needs time and attention.

These are some of the ground rules of
staying for the cup of coffee.

"Let me grieve the
way I need to. I don't
need to be rushed. I don't
need to meet expectations
put on me by others.
I need to do this my way.
This is my journey."

— Author unknown

Grief is healed through open and active mourning.

In other words, mourning is what gives grief momentum.

Every time you stay for the cup of coffee, you are creating conditions for one small burst of momentum to potentially be set in motion.

I call it "divine momentum" because it's a hopeful, spiritual blessing.

"Attention is the rarest and purest form of generosity."

— Simone Weil

MORE THINGS TO SAY

"I hear you."

"You're right—it doesn't seem _____
(fair, manageable, believable—reflecting something
the grieving person has expressed)."

"It's OK to _____ (cry, be angry,
be upset, have no energy, feel like you're
going crazy—normalizing something the
grieving person has expressed)."

"I'm honored to be your friend."

"Thank you for sharing with me."

"You matter to me."

Grief can feel very lonely.

On the inside, grieving people often feel immersed in
their loss. Their every thought and feeling may be either
about the loss or connected to the loss. This can go
on for a long time. Meanwhile, the outside world
goes on as if nothing has happened.

But!

But when you stop for the cup of coffee,
you are *not* continuing on as if nothing
has happened. Instead, you're acknowledging
that the loss needs attention, that the grieving person
needs others to pause with them.

You can help the person who is
grieving feel less alone.

Grace is being given
something good that you didn't earn
and maybe don't deserve.

Showing up for someone who's grieving
is an act of grace. You are offering
something good just because.

Just because you can.

Just because you care.

Just because it matters.

GRIEF CAFÉ

MENU

REFRESHMENTS
•
COMFORTABLE SEATING
•
PLEASANT ATMOSPHERE
•
SOMEWHERE THE GRIEVING PERSON
FEELS AT EASE
•
CONDUCIVE TO CONVERSATION
•
PRIVACY, if DESIRED
•
AMPLE TIME
•
LISTENING
•
EMPATHY

On mystical experiences

Loss can result in people having experiences
that are not always rationally explainable.
So, don't be surprised if the grieving person
shares mystical experiences with you.

Some grieving people talk about experiencing
visitations from the person who died. Sometimes
signs come in the forms of smells, sounds, or
natural phenomenon such as rainbows.

The grieving person is always the expert of
their own grief journey. If that journey includes
mystical experiences, that's OK.

Such understandings often give solace
and lend meaning. Your job is to deeply
listen and bring non-judgment.

Come bearing gifts

Your presence is always the most precious gift of all. But some people are also touched by thoughtful gifts.

Consider what the grieving person would enjoy, and bring something simple when you visit.

Vegetables from your garden

A package of a special tea or coffee

Something homemade, by you or by someone else

Cookies, muffins, or coffee cake

A book you love

A birdfeeder and seeds

Fresh flowers

A candle with a special scent

Lotion, bath salts, or other items for self-care

A cozy lap blanket

A fun or distracting toy, puzzle, or novelty item

You don't always have to stay for the cup of coffee.

In between coffee visits, it's helpful to simply check in with a quick text, phone call, or email.

"Just checking in."

"I saw _____ today and thought of you. How are you surviving?"

"You've been on my mind. When are you available to meet up for a coffee?"

"The sun feels wonderful today. Would you like to go for a short walk with me?"

"I made a giant batch of (soup, lasagna, hummus, etc.). I'd like to drop some off for you this afternoon."

"I just watched a movie and thought you might like it."

"Whatever happened with _____ (following up on something)?"

"Care for a quick visit?"

"Let's get together to watch the game. Are you up for it?"

The longer I live,
the more deeply I learn that love—
whether we call it friendship or
family or romance—is the work of
mirroring and magnifying
each other's light."

— James Baldwin

You might feel that you're not a natural at empathy. Maybe you're not that good at staying for the cup of coffee.

Don't let this stop you from reaching out. Because even if your attempts to support the grieving person are tentative or far from perfect, they'll understand that you're expressing your love and trying to help.

Studies have shown that people appreciate overtures of support—even awkward ones. Simply by showing up and being yourself, you're doing what's most needed.

OFFER CARE THAT ONLY YOU CAN OFFER

My three-phase mantra for being
present to others in grief:

No rewards for speed.

Not attached to outcome.

Divine momentum.

I repeat these phrases silently to myself
for a few minutes before meeting
with a grieving person.

When you're spending time with the grieving person, remember

the power of the open-ended question.

Open-ended questions are those that require more than a yes or no answer. They encourage the grieving person to open up and share.

Then what happened?

How are you surviving?

What has been worrying you?

What do you think/how do you feel?

Tell me everything.

SPRINKLE EVERYTHING WITH KINDNESS

"Listening is being able to be changed by the other person."

— Alan Alda

On prayer

Some grieving people find solace and
meaning in prayer. Some do not.

Your goal is to support the grieving person,
so follow their lead on this.

If they indicate that they find prayer meaningful,
then it may help them to know you're praying for them
or that you've added their name to a prayer list.

If, on the other hand, you learn that they find "thoughts
and prayers" empty or frustrating, don't mention prayer.

**As always, your support should center on the
needs and beliefs of the grieving person.**

Making meaning

What gives life meaning? The grieving person is probably wondering this.

After all, a relationship that gave their life meaning has ended. What now?

Now here you come to offer your time and compassion.

You are not the "answer" to the grieving person's questions about meaning and purpose. But you *are* here to show your support and remind them that they still have people in their life who care.

Don't make the mistake of thinking that staying for the cup of coffee is an empty social norm. It's not.

It's a sacred ritual that helps the grieving person find meaning and purpose again.

DON'T BE SURPRISED

If you're one of the few people who gets the importance of staying for the cup of coffee.

If the grieving person tells you they have nobody else to talk to.

If a grieving person you assumed was well-supported isn't.

If the grieving person shares thoughts and feelings with you that they've never shared with anyone else.

If you develop a deeper friendship.

If, for a while, you play a big part in helping the grieving person survive.

If your steadfast support makes all the difference.

Hard days

Consider staying for the cup of coffee on or around some of the hardest days:

- the anniversary of the death
- the birthday of the person who died or the grieving person
- holidays
- special family dates, such as wedding anniversaries

When you're grieving, any day can be hard, but these days are often harder.

Start a tradition

Staying for the cup of coffee is a
time-honored social ritual.

But you and the grieving person can create your
own ritual—one that suits the two of you.

Maybe you get together for lunch on the
first Wednesday of each month.

Maybe you go for a walk or play golf
together on Friday afternoons.

Maybe you regularly do a certain activity side by side,
such as knitting or watching football.

Carve out a special time and place and stick to it.

Grief requires outward expression, or mourning. But it also requires inward reflection and solitude.

Sometimes the grieving person might ask to be left alone. If so, that's OK.

Your purpose is to stay for the cup of coffee when they're open to your companionship. And to keep offering to stay for the cup of coffee until they're ready.

It's normal for self-care to slip in early grief.

If your grieving friend isn't eating well
or is wearing the same clothes all the time
or has lowered their hygiene
standards, that's normal.

But over time, because you're continuing to
stay for the cup of coffee, you can monitor their
self-care. Some grieving people slide into clinical
depression. Others experience a worsening of
health problems because they're not taking their
medication or drinking enough water.

If the grieving person's self-care becomes
alarmingly worrisome, it may be time for
you to step in and talk to them about
getting more support.

OFFER ONE OR TWO

When you hold space for someone who's grieving, you're not only letting them know you care.

You're also letting them know that
they're worth it.

They are worthy of:

unconditional support

attention

compassion

time

true friendship

LEND A HELPING HAND

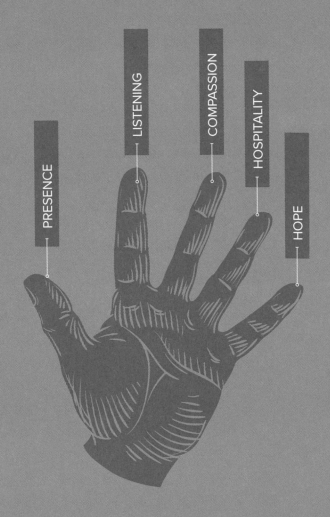

PRESENCE

LISTENING

COMPASSION

HOSPITALITY

HOPE

When you're staying for the cup of coffee
with a grieving friend, you might put your

foot in your mouth.

You might say something judgmental,
ill-advised, or unkind.

You might change the subject if the
conversation gets too raw.

You might get distracted by your phone or
pulled away by other demands.

 **If you make a mistake, that's OK.
Staying for the cup of coffee honors
the full range of human experience.**

Simply acknowledge your gaffe and apologize.
Re-emphasize your desire to help.

Your space as refuge

Sometimes grieving people become hermits.
They're wounded, and while they're
convalescing, feel safer at home.

But sometimes they need help getting out and
about again. Grieving people can get stuck.

You can make your home a hospitable,
safe place for them to begin venturing out.
Your home can also provide them with a
needed change of venue, an unsticking of
patterns that may have grown unhealthy.

Invite the grieving person over for coffee.
Help them re-engage with life.

"The quieter you become, the more you are able to hear."

— Rumi

Judgment

Shame

Abandonment

Looking away

Respect

Affirmation

Staying for the cup of coffee

Bearing witness

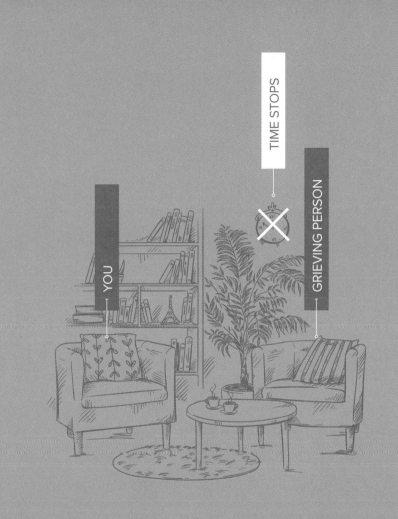

TIME STOPS

YOU

GRIEVING PERSON

If the grieving person needs more help

You might find that the grieving person needs more help than you alone can provide.

Traumatic loss circumstances, personality issues, substance use disorders, concurrent life stressors, mental health challenges—these and other factors can turn normal grief into complicated grief.

If you see something, say something. Talk to the grieving person about your concerns. Share your concerns with others when appropriate.

Help the grieving person reach out to get the additional support they need.

GRATITUDE

Of course, you don't stay for the cup of coffee because you expect gratitude.

You do it because **you're** grateful.

**Grateful for this opportunity to
be a good friend.**

**Grateful for the chance to make a
difference in someone's life.**

Grateful that all it takes is showing up.

Grieving people often can't see the progress they're making. They're still mired in too much pain.

So go ahead and
point out progress
when you notice it.

"You've survived X weeks/months already."

"You've started walking/gardening/
playing golf again."

"I love seeing you laugh again."

"You're really enjoying _____."

"(Name of person who died) would be so happy/
proud to see you _____."

"You're allowing yourself to go backward
so you can eventually go forward."

"I'm so impressed that you've learned to
_____."

"Listening is a magnetic and strange thing, a creative force. The friends who listen to us are the ones we move toward. When we are listened to, it creates us, makes us unfold and expand."

— Karl A. Menninger

"It is only when you learn to be present and available with non-judgment and compassionately hold space for the wounded and broken fragments of yourself that you are able to truly hold space for another."

— Markus William Kasunich

Validate, validate, validate

People in pain appreciate
acknowledgment of their pain.

A simple act of validation can
make all the difference.

"What a difficult time you're going through."

"I can hear how much you're hurting."

"Help me understand how you're really doing."

"It seems like you're really _____
(sad, angry, lost, lonely, afraid)."

"Things are really rough for you right now.
What can I do to help?"

Staying for the cup of coffee works best if the grieving person has multiple people in their life who offer the same kind of support.

Consider finding out who else is staying for the cup of coffee in the grieving person's life.

If you have mutual friends or family members, it may be appropriate for you to help educate a few of them about the practice and importance of staying for the cup of coffee.

Most people want to help but don't know how. You can teach them.

"You will never forget a person who came to you with a torch in the dark."

— M. Rose

Progress in the grief journey is naturally slow and halting. Sometimes it's two steps forward, one step back.

And remember, there are no rewards for speed. (In fact, what looks like fast healing can be ongoing numbness or denial.)

Over time, and with your ongoing support, you may notice **SIGNS OF HEALING** begin to emerge:

A feeling of release from the person who died. The love and attachment are still there, but the grieving person is no longer preoccupied by the loss.

A return to stable eating and sleeping patterns.

The enjoyment of experiences in life that are normally enjoyable.

The awareness that one doesn't "get over" grief but instead learns to live with the new reality.

The drive to organize and plan life toward to the future.

A sense of renewed meaning and purpose.

Does simply being there
for the grieving person
really help?

Yes.

Thank you for being a good friend in grief.

Thank you for showing up,
being present, and holding space.

Thank you for making the world a better place.

Thank you for being one of those who care.
As fellow human beings, we cannot cure,
but we can always care.

THANK YOU FOR STAYING FOR THE CUP OF COFFEE.

I hope we meet one day.